A BRIGHT ACOUSTIC

Philip Gross was born in 1952 in Delabole, Cornwall. Since winning a Gregory Award in 1981 and first prize in the National Poetry Competition in 1982 he has published books with Peterloo, Faber and Bloodaxe, including *The Air Mines of Mistila*, with Sylvia Kantaris (1988: Poetry Book Society Choice), *The Wasting Game* (1998) and *Changes of Address: Poems 1980-1998* (2001). His later books include *A Bright Acoustic* (2017); *Love Songs of Carbon* (2015), PBS Recommendation and winner of the Roland Mathias Poetry Award (Wales Book of the Year); *Later* (2013); *Deep Field* (2011), a PBS Recommendation; *The Water Table* (2009), winner of the T.S. Eliot Prize; *The Egg of Zero* (2006); and *Mappa Mundi* (2003), a PBS Recommendation – all from Bloodaxe. His collaborations include *A Fold in the River* (Seren, 2015) with artist Valerie Coffin Price, and *I Spy Pinhole Eye* (Cinnamon Press, 2009) with photographer Simon Denison, which won the Wales Book of the Year Award 2010.

His poetry for children includes *Manifold Manor*, *The All-Nite Café* (winner of the Signal Award 1994), *Scratch City* and *Off Road To Everywhere* (winner of the CLPE Award 2011). He has published ten novels for young people, most recently *The Storm Garden* (2006), and wrote the libretto for *The King in the Car Park*, a cantata about Richard III, performed by three hundred schoolchildren in Leicester Cathedral.

He has taught writing at every step on the educational ladder from nursery to PhD, and relishes collaboration with musicians, dancers and visual artists of all kinds. A Quaker who has also written horror and science fiction, he lives with his wife Zélie in Penarth in South Wales.

PHILIP GROSS

A Bright Acoustic

BLOODAXE BOOKS

Copyright © Philip Gross 2017

ISBN: 978 1 78037 368 3

First published 2017 by
Bloodaxe Books Ltd,
Eastburn,
South Park,
Hexham,
Northumberland NE46 1BS.

www.bloodaxebooks.com
For further information about Bloodaxe titles
please visit our website or write to
the above address for a catalogue.

Supported using public funding by
ARTS COUNCIL
ENGLAND

Cover design: Neil Astley & Pamela Robertson-Pearce.

Printed in Great Britain by Bell & Bain Limited, Glasgow, Scotland, on
acid-free paper sourced from mills with FSC chain of custody certification.

for the many others, living and dead,
with whom these poems are a conversation

ACKNOWLEDGEMENTS

Acknowledgements are due to: *A Festschift for Tony Frazer, Amsterdam Review, English, Geohumanities, International Literary Quarterly, Journal of Arts and Communities, Manhattan Review, New Welsh Reader, New Writing: The International Journal for the Practice and Theory of Creative Writing, Poetry Daily, The Poetry Review, RSPB Anthology of Wildlife Poetry, Scintilla, The High Window, The Reader*; and to Manchester University Press for poems included in *Halfway-to-Whole Things: Ecologies of Writing and Collaboration* in *Extending Ecocriticism*, ed. Peter Barry.

Some of the poems appeared in *Time in the Dingle*, IPSI Chapbook 1 (International Poetry Studies Institute, University of Canberra, 2015). 'Applause, Applause' was commissioned by *Festival of Sound: The Sound of English Poetry*, Magdalene College, Cambridge. The Heraclitus variations formed the text of *Flow & Frame*, a poetry-film collaboration with Wyn Mason and Kevin Mills.

CONTENTS

Clarity

In the sense of transparence,
I don't mean that much can be explained

Clarity in the sense of silence.

GEORGE OPPEN, 'Of Being Numerous'

Windfarm at Sea

Wind flowers
in the mist
as if dark-grown, as spindly as whims,

off the grey coast where there's no horizon
but one we infer, where they walk

or sleepwalk, in their middle distance
of just-possibility

considering all this
in their absent and abstracted way,

three-petalled, unpeeling themselves: loves me
loves me not – unpicking the knot of the winds,

a twist of faded ribbon tied round the idea,
no more than that,

of the trunk of a tree...
as if we'd stumbled on the pale machinery

that drives the weather, the obsession
in it, like the distance at the heart

of too much love. Like a stalker
in love with a ghost.
Like a wedding in grey.

Not the sound, but the texture

of sound on the water... as a low-
        hung mud-
encrusted dredger leaves the docks

        a mile off; its thrum
is here before it, a drub-a-dub

kneading of the bottom edge

of hearing, wave forms almost
        still and visible

like small barkhans of beach
    drift stopped
in fossil strata in the mudstone cliffs

        of here and now. (Now,
crumbling, always.) It's the rub

of surfaces, of one against the other,

air on water, as the earth, that rare
        old globe of fluids,

        slops, eddies and flows –
a swishing tail of jet stream or crusts
        riding and buckling, sucking

under, fast or slow, depending
        on your distance: here,

with your ear to the ground

        or the sea or the thrub
of the blood in your veins, the heart's

machinery, this almost
music, heard as if far out and off
across wide water.

Mew

1

These sheer,
these curling sound-flakes
    gulls slice off the air
like a chef nuancing an onion, so
wincingly thin they're near
transparent, so deft
    it's a blur...
Just the sound of it, just remembering,
    my eyes sting.

2

Inland, at the landfill, they chuck,
    squabble, gossip – not this,
        not the sea-
    cry, untranslatable
in any human language, equally.

3

Mob-handed, they're rigging the air
with cries like hawsers, like high-tensile steel
    – the great construction project
        of the moment. Which comes
        crashing all around us
        gloriously.

4

It's all echo – the sound of the sound
barrier broken, you might think
forever, not a boom
                but this brilliant

shatter, a ram-raid on silence, flying
splinters of glass each with the sky
still in them, like the chandelier's

most thrilling nightmare, or an ice
cave in an earthquake, and it's only

3.27, teatime, Thursday afternoon.

5

Their voices
have already left them:
distance, come too close for comfort

at the window. We are mewed in.

What they say
does not bear thinking.
Give it houseroom, give it too much mind,

it will take you away.

Time in the Dingle

Mist in the dingle

and the still-bare branches
not so much seen through
      as inscribed

in frosted glass.
         Every single
thing close; you could wipe it away.
            One touch –
all this might undo itself, gather and run.

Glassy, too, the acoustic.
         Each droplet
like a hanging splinter, glinting
              not with light
but sound, each bird-pitch, sudden, there

and there. And shattered: that's
how brittle our time is
      – hung

(we can guess but not see)
           in the act
of dissolution, its crystalline structure
              still in place,
in space: a small universe, in which each

from every other particle
         is always turning,
as if every possible spot
            was an exit,
to go.

*

Their soundings

see through walls – thicker than walls,
the chain-mail darkness of inside the yew,
the holly, the dust-sheet drapes of ivy,

inwardness which only intricately
niggled gimlet-pricks of light get through.

And yet the plump and sudden…what?

hedge sparrows? seem to pass
at a tilt, a hurtle, without let or hindrance.

Or they hold still, fill
the whole bush with their stillness –
just the ping-trace of their calls

to stitch the world together, space
to matter, and their own,

each other's, place in it.

*

The dingle, sunlit

: photosynthesis factory,
        all silent-
            whirring cogs
of its chlorophyll cells,

a shop floor in the sky.

And equally, a high-
        hall banquet,
            crowd of waiters

balancing around each other

with their trays of light.

*

Sounds

       pretty, doesn't it? Like the word,
the one I'm squirming to avoid; I've tried cleft
cleave coomb chine for this sudden steep slip

       of a strip of stray wildwood
into this crack crease interstice slightly
unpicked seam between breezeblock railing fence

       over which, not quite concealed
by under-tangle, small spews of rubbish get spilled
as if over-the-hedge was outside-of-the-story

       and into hiatus, the kind of between
we make with backs turned, where a place, a whole
order of things, might absent abscond conceal

       itself under a word like
dingle – there, I've said it. Yap-dog in the leaf-mould.
We can call its name but it won't come to heel.

*

A memory, then,

one in the present tense,
of a stream that cut this steep –

18

sweet water ships put in for.
Half its catchment gone

into gutters and storm drains,
what's left seeps

to a mud pool. No visible flow.
But look, we can't resist it,

the offering: cans, parking cones,
any Saturday night; a sign, once,

for *Residents Only*. Mud:
something richer

than mere jinks or grievance, something
knowing, and that will

outlast us, with a wink of wit.

*

The dingle, rain

Lip over lap, the fifty feet of broadleaf. It's a rain
intensifier. Drifting mist-condition up above
is recollected downwards
                              leaf by leaf,
pooled, runnelled. Pondered, into droplets.
Every now and then one strikes you
like a bon mot (too
                      considered), like an anecdote.

*

Dawn

chorus...? No, rather the clatter of toolkits
     on echoing floorboards,
the measuring up of spaces in the day:
     the long ticking out
and snick back of a metal inch-tape,
then the tiny power tools out again.

Or earlier, the day still on the drawing board:
     the architects, extrapolating vectors.
Calculus of sound. An audible force diagram
     inked on the air. Close your eyes,
see it as dim blue-glowing graphics you can turn
and flex through three dimensions. Only

you are absent, you, dark matter, moving through
     that matrix, to be known
by the way the space distorts around you
     as you pass. Your only power:
to be the dumbness into which their sound
collapses. (All around you now, its splintering.)

To be the blind spot, larger today. And one day
     there's the whole wood, gone.

*

Gone

     Imagine that.

The sound of it.
Air's harp unstrung.

          A great
          unlistening.

*

In his last year

he walked this way, daily. Nothing scared,
nothing startled, shrilled or jangled its alarm.

He made no dent in the air.

Though no one knew yet, he'd already gone that far.

*

To the birds

in the three dimensions of the dingle
I am flatfoot
down here in the silt.

At their pitch I am low
as underground, the premonition
of an earthquake. In their time I am slow

as a trilobite shuffling to my station
in Jurassic mudstone
even when I think I'm running for the train.

*

…or the squirrel

who's only at home in the vertical

(*contra* gravity: look,

he pours up, up a fifty-foot oak as if I'd spilled him)

– or at ease
on the high wire stretched

from one last twig tip to the next by fine momentum.

On the ground
he's twitchy, first frozen

then panicky,
as if living in the horizontal gave him vertigo.

*

Should I try

to call them by their names: dun
dunnock, mouse-wren, those dim pigeons on the cusp
between plumpness and panic, blackbird
of the quick askance look in its gold rimmed specs?

But there's nothing to say

half so resonant as this untenanted
attic that's home to their voices, or the slip-
stream of some body leaving
just its disembodied sound print on the world.

Besides, would they do the same for me?

Well, there may be a tweak
or a cant in the timbre of the shrills
that shiver out round me this evening
where I've trespassed, here… while there

a differently-pitched clangour spreads this way

down the path towards me, from where
at the corner, a single-shade-darker-
than-dusk slim fox
has stopped, appraising,

then drops to a fast low level scurry

right by, almost through me, yielding
nothing, not at this hour, as if I
was a rumour that's abroad
but better not believed.

*

Jaunty and Jack-

the-laddish, the voice of jackdaws...
We say *voice*. Crows, harsher, scathing,
one step closer to the raven's *Doom*...

Whereas those giggle-twitters,
those tweedle-dumb
tit-flocks always on a spree,

are charming, aren't they? (Just because
a station, Larks FM, goes out on shorter
wavelengths, do we think it's cute?)

*

Dark, now,

the under-layer of its sound,
its quiet too, is water.

Less than trickle or drip.

Its slight release.
                    Inaudible

by day, now its percussions,
the snicks of a jeweller's hammer,
the cogs that work its small
                    accommodations to itself,

emerge like the first stars
in a night sky that, beyond
leaf cover and the tea-stain ochre
of a city's slow light-leakage, don't
                    care whether anybody looks to see.

*

It takes me out

of myself, he would say. Stopped
mid walk, mid step almost, following
each chink of sound, all at once
to its several source.
The unseen.

Spreading out, the spaces in him,
between thought and thought and
himself, into a great
dispersion.

When the time comes, scatter me.

*

Today, I'm with the wind

all the way. Rip it up, the dingle. Right down
to the roots. I'm with the wind as it bends, bends

24

back and forth and back, fatigue lines thickening

till you can hear it, the crackling relinquishment,
the crumbling at the root tips, at the point
each one chooses to slip free or snap

in a scatter of earth, the handful on the coffin lid.
Lever the whole show up, crown, underlay and all,
leaving a gape in the topsoil, an opencast,

for the wind to scratch at, still baffled
by this urge to rip up, baffled by itself.

*

One down

is the sum of it. One root-ball come unknit
from the long consensus, one full-length sprawl
into the horizontal

and the hundred-year-old railings buckled
under and about. The footpath taped off
like an Incident.

Already, at first light, the chainsaw gang is up,
humming into the job of subdivision:
ripe metre-thick steaks

of bole like gossip, oven-ready; each bare-
faced slice of rings a still-shocked version
of the same old story.

*

Fractal

(Compare the collateral wreck
        of a smashed bough – *shivered* –

divorced from itself, cell by cell
        at unknowable junctures.
Just measure the surface of that,

yes, down to fractal levels: laid
        flat, ironed to a sheet of no depth

it could wrap itself, the whole
        place and me gently and fold
us away, maybe for mending later.)

*

Precipitation

within sight… that's so fine
it seems not to be falling

but condensing from the air
at each (sharp) point.

The orange streetlamp's part of it, the mist
and its solution,

just subtracting here and there a twig-
tip perfect silhouette

like someone or something
best remembered

being gone.

*

A damp May morning,

> cleared...
> to the birds, to an open-
> plan office, with squeaky-
clean panes of something we can't see,
to its glassy part-partitions, its negotiations, its
insider dealings, its yes
> yes, its professional
> call-centre cheer.

*

The myth

the metaphor, that this is music...
Just because our toys (the bone flute

from a cave bear femur, or the first
time a boy feels a grass blade shriek

between his thumbs) approximate
to the sounds of the forest machine

– cogs in operation; the friction
as much as the mesh is what we hear.

Or the creak of the world's pipes,
morning, evening, its small seasons:

the rough adjustments of space
against space, warping

the matter round it. Stress patterns
that it pleases us to hear as harmonies.

*

It writes itself,

the dingle: scribble-pad
for the hithering-thithering
gnat flecks, the hoverflies'
quiver and twitch,
                        some stray
imago flipped like a silvery
5p, heads-tails, into day-
long life...
                Praise be
to God's rough workings,
sometimes bird-snack, some-
times intersecting, in a brief
spark, with a squint of light.

*

Two brown butterflies

dropped into the sunlight, whirling, dizzily

entangled without touching, in their tight
and wonky orbits, wobbling

electrons making something out of nothing, almost

without substance, almost without colour in their blur,
such flimsies, helpless in the force

that makes the whole show spin and hum.

*

This kind of drizzle-
                    damp, then,
is a keeper
        of each least chink
and sip and whim of sound;

relays it inwards, each
droplet to each
                and to each,
their micro-circuitry

that might be a recording,
if we had a way
                to play it;
meanwhile, is a white-

noise curtain drawn around
you being
        here, today,
this circumstance,

this afternoon, what's left of it
at four pm,
            December, never
generous, but keeping something

for itself and those who know it.
Depth,
        in no direction.
A mute introspection of light.

*

It's a body,

                this dingle, as real as my own
with one skin upwards, sunwards, at the canopy
or a little above, in the thrill of small insects.
Leaf-breath, leaf-sweat. Now and then a bird
breaks cover, comes and goes
                          as do our own
constituents, could we but see it. Where
the lower skin senses is nowhere we can go,
beyond the subtlest root-hairs. Down-drainage.
up-seepage, capillary thirst.
                      In between,
pulled open by opposing tractions...space,
a gasp, shapeless at first, then shuddering
with small vibrations, now and then a voice,
even that, even mine...
                  who fools himself
he's other, an observer – rather than a thought
the dingle has, that passes through its body
forming into 'now'... dispersing into 'here'...
this creak, this yelp, this
                  twitter, 'me...'

*

And don't neglect

the smells, though neglect is what they thrive on:

a whole dinner service, heaped plates,
of the bracket fungus on the tree that fell two years ago

and has been rotting for them, ready,
at first saffron, glowing from the skylight
that its rift made in the canopy,

now bruising to black. The deep
nutritious mould smells rising,

like the mirror image in another sense
of how our minds are elsewhere. In-
attention. The ripe fruit of it.

*

Before night

folds the dingle inwards,
page to page and ink to ink...

on a branch, only just
above head height, a blunt

stump of shadow   shifts
to an owl-silhouette,

appraising me, I him. I think
words, when the book shuts,

read each other   in the darkness,
close as close and inside out and back to front.

*

November, now

: the leaves fall through
      the wood, not in it
           / under / from it.
Or it draws itself up, the dingle, up and in,
a little straighter
      in a shower of gravity;

knows itself more, or
more precisely, the barer, the less, it becomes.

*

All the contraries,

at play, in the dingle... Things it wants to be:
a busy lull, an airy womb filled with a shudder-
pulse of green,
                  both too quick and too slow
to grasp by looking – listen, there's a depth
            above us – a snug vertigo
with, now, that single bird-blip: the affectless
curiosity
            of sonar. It will find us.
                                        Space
too close, sometimes, too pressing in,
almost, to bear... Something

that's beginning, always,
                              even as it ends.

*

Who,

If I cried out, would hear me...?
                              Rilke, if that's a plea,
then no, not the birds any more than your angels,

not this unseen host, this constellation
of bright points of presence. What brings me

or you or anybody to a cry
means nothing in this bird-space, tree-space, prey-

or hunter-space except... attend
a moment: danger? or advantage? Then it could go on

(*Fling this emptiness / out of your arms,*
Back into the spaces/ into which we breathe...)

unhindered: human weeping, wind, a distant
playground clangour soft as leaf fall, passing siren, rain.

*

Leaf blowers

against the wind. Me too they give a quick whirl sideways,
set me at a different angle to myself

with a wry half grin, half salute, from the man with the fat
bazooka-blower, his mate with the rake

and bin bag, either side of the path like Gog and Magog.
Not much future in this occupation

so hey, no hurry either, here with autumn rising
on the wind-tide, just about to flood.

*

Exotic:

bamboo too – yes, here among the ivy – refugee
         from someone's dream of elsewhere.
                  Rife, be-wildered.
         Here's an end to travels. Good
or bad news, there is nowhere else you need to go.

*

Wren Time

Flitter-flicked, the blur and gone
of it, at ankle height... and me
in mid step – stilled.
                                Wren
like a new proposition: that

this wood
                (timed to its heart
beat, its wing beat)
                                is strung
with gloopy swags of bird song:

blackbird slow and heavy as velvet
stage drapes –
                        or the dustbin-lid alarm
spreading out in thick ripples
as I lumber into view.
                                The wren's

gift: to expose, in a tick,
the moment's architecture, spacious,
ripe for living in
                        (though not
for me; I'm heavy weather, merely)

by lives that set foot on its girders
as lightly as the Mohawks
riveting Manhattan
                                to the sky
paused, posed and

grinning at the camera's
hand-shake, scattering
                                their grins
and lunch crumbs to the heedless
streets below.

Back

Just a wish out of place – the first click
    starts a ticking backwards: one pop of a pod
        of balsam, like a caught breath, like a sigh

in-sucked, and its blush-blooms, in popsicle-pink
    and all over us briefly, start acting their age
        now, retracting their flip asides; they shrink

into something like shame. Go dark
    like a playhouse in Puritan times. The buddleia
        shrugs off its easy disconnected butterflies.

But this will be nothing to the tearing
    up, the snap-crackling of roots. First that sad
        defeated carnival of rhododendrons (and who

would defend *them*?) herded from the hills; then
    the other non-natives, one by one… The pears
        may try to merge in with the apples, yes,

the crabbiest of them, until they're denounced
    and we'll wake to the rumble of the sycamores
        retreating; London planes stripped of the name,

leaving squares bare and pitted. They make for the sea,
    hoping to unpick the trade routes, wind the tides
        back, all the accidents that brought them…

Now the lights are going out all over
    Europe's gardens. Bird migrations locked out.
        Silence deep enough to catch the drift

like smoke, like snow, of the murmur of *gone*
    approaching: wildfowl flowing south, the grunt
        and lowing of the ice sheet crumpling into place.

Almost as if we'd wished it. As if it had never been away.

Ten Takes on the Garden

It could, I quite see, grow on you:
the seduction of melancholy. A deciduous
emotion, longing to be mulch.

*

The corkscrew willow: every inch a nervous tic.
How much of what we prize –
Exquisite! – is deformity?

*

Or the shrill of a New England (dying,
dying) Fall – its annual opera. Car-loads
turn out to be ravished by magnificent distress.

*

A *garden inclos'd*... Outside, the soft
lathe-hum of traffic is part of the point:
that is there. And therefore: this is here...

*

... which might be tragic, if we didn't half
believe *this* is the real, right world – the rest,
at best, approximation and at worst, mistake.

*

The mechanical birds of the Great Khan's
pleasure garden? We have moorhens
ticking over the pond, with rusty squeaks.

*

How subtly crushing is the ruthless calm
of ducks (when they're not panicking,
that is). We are dismissed by it.

*

And as for Nature? Where more satisfied
than this: the cut stump rotting, liquefying almost,
larvae hard at work on softness, little guts.

*

Where were we? Treading water.
Damp rises. Gravity sucks. And we're busy
just keeping our heads above ground.

*

When the wind blows, rashly coloured scraps
of children scatter in among the leaves
or vice versa, who knows which is which.

Twenty Questions about Green

1. What, so close to the thickening heart-knot of the country's motorways, could be the meaning of this garden – the meaning of green?

2. Is a lawn an exercise – yes, and a groundsman's labour – in concentrating all our minds on that: clipped, kept, to concentrate its colour: green?

3. What is it we feel, even if it isn't our own memory, is being remembered by this gathered meeting of a hundred greens?

4. How far back do we have to peel the history before the water, the brook in the wood, would recognise its 'own face before it was born'?

5. And if it did, would it have anything to say to us any more, or be off, in itself, and away?

6. Does it mind, this water, that we have detained it here, delayed it on its way, to call it 'lake'?

7. And the dragonfly's glint, which was metallic before we had metal, the damselfly's, neon before neon, whose dream is that: ours, the water's or their own?

8. Are they better off not to be weighed down with memories – of the great dragonflies, say, of the Carboniferous, not yet come down to our time's jewelled toys?

9. But when did the concept of *lawn* first step out of the trees, onto the stage of itself, and take a bow?

10. Something might safely graze, it whispers to our Sunday School selves – ah, but what, or who?

11. How much closer might I get to *that*, what as kids we called Dinosaur Rhubarb, if I knew its proper name?

12. Or if I knew that name – which it, itself, does not – how much further apart might we be?

13. What shuffling and dealing took place round the edges of their habits, so many species, before their ornamental rooming-house became a home?

14. And if we should turn our back on them for a year, for ten, for a hundred, what would the meaning of green be then?

15. How much more of the brown, the greyish, the mould-blue, the lichen-yellow, does there truly want to be?

16. Isn't green itself a strenuous gesture, all that striving for the sunlight, just another kind of hungering?

17. If we ask every species here to name itself to us, just once, in the language in which anyone or thing first named them, do we have ears to hear?

18. Could we bear it, that awful laying-down of language, uncountable as leaves themselves, as dying, at our feet?

19. What might we be asked to lay at *their* feet, roots and tendrils, in return?

20. And when we did, when we stepped out, over it, into the silence, into green, together, then what would we be?

A Cult of Bees

Today she rises and she dresses.
Every one of us is her attendant in the robing room –

drone, worker, even the queen.
Every drop squeezed from our bodies, wax and honey,

is to fashion her a body,
a shape in this world, and it glows, as if she was the one

true candle, of which all
your candles are the stray reflections, very far and small.

Today she rises and will be robed
in our wings, spun pearl, which we shed for her gladly,

strew them at her feet like petals.
We lay out our bodies, scattered on the orchard floor,

swept out of doors of the hive.
We are her feelers, glands and limbs. We have no word

for what we, each by each,
might be, as ready for the journey now she rises,

and we clothe her with ourselves.
She is nothing, and all that we are: the ungraspable pattern

in the live brocade of swarming,
the shapes that we trace in the air, always threading our amber

beads on their string. She
is... But ask your candle, in its whispering under the breath

of the flame. She cares
for everything, and cares for nothing. She is not for you.

Ear Candle

(for Jon and Petra)

A word in your ear – and the word is
candle. A pale stalk of beeswax
like the oil refinery's
slim stack

across the marshes, when by night its single petal
flickers. That balancing trick.
If it's a tongue,

this flame, it's lascivious, inconstant
yet brisk... Just a lick on the air,
on a thought, it's sealed
and posted, there

gone already, up into the world of weather,
where everything lives at its
no-fixed-address.

I'd thought the point might be the whispering,
of comfort maybe, rather than this
in-breath, this drawing up
and out what

entered – day's clatter, the chitter-and-shuffling
impacts, their repercussions in echoing
hangar darkness,

tanks and girders (tiny anvil still distantly
clanging at all hours) as the night
shift cleaners clock in,
sluicing ducts

and drums, with no more force than this,
the up-suck of a candle – how
it might tease out a strand

                              of my time, like tangled string, unbraid it
                                    into smoke, a million-bat flock
                                        unfurling, undoing itself
                                            from the cave,

dispersing, from matter to vapour, to sky,
and there's a word for that
too: *sublimate*.

Danseuse Cambodgienne

... whom Rodin, sixty-six
and stiff already, caught – not her but

windrush in her wake, her tracks in space-
time: each movement an already-

absence, a trace in the cloud chamber.
She is there

only approximately, ever: split
particles spin into the no-time-

ever-after, small worlds
steady in the orbit

of a three-day dervish trance.
She's a scribble

of data leaking into hearsay, indo-
chinese whispers: where she *is*

is immaterial
while, watching, he's

the room's fug, he's a blur.
Is smoke. She flares.

Is wind. Is almost
hypothetical. Is nothing

but a footnote, him
a footnote to the footnote,

to the real thing, the dance.

A Cadence:

the slack-jointed run
      of the young skateboarder off

the precinct ramp, with a kick

to mount the kerb, along/atop
      a low wall, barely slowing –

eyes down, not so much on his feet

as in his body, more haste in the flapping
      of his loose tee, or his bum-hung britches

than the slow long stoop and push

of each pulse of his glide
      to an inch from the drop

where the wall ends; with barely a twitch

he's tripped up the board-tip
      so it spins free, him

in mid stride now without it, to land

as it offers itself to his hand
      just snug to deal on

to the pavement where his next

step delivers them
      together, a descending

grace-note, to the theme...

Stylus

Not with a bang, but with a dull
cthunk of the autochanger. Then the hiss
    (hiss with a waver in it)
       of beginning
soon... This would be not long after time began,
time as a number, as the still pool of everything
    so far snapped over the weir
       into a new decade.

I heard it rushing in the hiss; the clunky
Dansette arm bucked slightly, the stylus (and this
    was the wonder I had to believe)
       alive, they said, in two
dimensions so that we could hear in three.
Stylus: a shred of tin with a fang on it, a tiny
    diamond. Then I closed my eyes
       and fell

through impossible space. Into *stereo*.
The first time. In some nowhere in between
    the wardrobe and my shrug-hung
       blue plaid dressing-gown,
my school bag next to it, by my *Look and Learn*
pull-out Solar System (seen from the sidelines,
    keeping Pluto company)
       the ungraspable thing,

music, was teetering up – years on, maybe a lark
ascending; then, Hank Marvin's one-string solo
    deft work with the tremolo arm
       made shivery,
up out of sight and hearing, somewhere
where I spread out with it into nothing, or
    was it that the distance
       opened

deeper than I could hold... but inside me?

The Breath of Things

despite themselves: the tight brief wheeze
        of air brakes, no sooner applied
than insisted on, no sooner that than released
        like a firm teacher's grip on the class,
                her flicker of I *mean it*.
                    (Tactful, too,
like a too-well-brought-up great aunt's painful tiny sneeze.)

*

So many things, not just those aimed at heaven,
        have that leaky harmonium sound;
            the Spirit limps in
with its old touch of emphysema, settles
        in a back pew, sets
the rusty corrugated tabernacle ringing
            with a hymn.

*

Or under King's Cross, catch the overlapping sigh-
        sighs of a tube train braking
as the platform, its lit flicker-book of posters,
        faces, slows and slows:
wave under wave of pressure not let go
        but finessed to a standstill... then,
hand over hand, climbs into speed, us with it, in the dark again.

*

'An exhalation of the earth':
            think, if mist
had a voice, if we could thin ourselves to subtlety
        enough to hear it... Think
how intimate, how close to the skin
        on all sides, how
as if it really loved us it would breathe.

*

There are extremes, barely liveable. Winds of the steppe
　　　　in the throat-singer's body, somewhere:
heights and depths no body can contain. (They are said
　　　　　　　to die young.) The hound
crouched, a breath rumbling. Meanwhile, that wild
　　　　held whine, like a hawk in its jesses.
Silk kite on a taut string, flexing, whickering.

*

Beyond voice, like a runner sagging to his knees
　　　　with the news he can't utter, a meaning
　　　　　　　that the body only knows
　　　　and can't support – beyond
it mattering, whose victory and whose defeat.
　　　　　　　　Pure breath.
Always an expiration, in the end.

*

Reaching the outer shore of breath – beyond
　　　　here, the true ocean –
on the long strand: footsteps with a hollow, glassy sound
fall into rhythm of the clutch and the straggling sigh-
　　　　release of waves on shingle. Of shingle
on wave. Beyond this point there is no difference
　　　　　　what, who, which on which.

*

Your breath, beside me in the dark,
　　　　　　has a hitch.
　　　　No efficient machine,
our breathing grazes, rather, skimming off some oxygen.
　　　　Fire does this better. We laze a while
on the bank, trailing fingers, weed-fronds of our bronchioles,
in the clear running stream of the air.

Tír na nÓg

: these stray islands of light in the middle of the seaway
       – never inhabited, naturally,
            unless by creatures of light
who've no truck with our comings and goings, ages,
       humours, our container hulks
            low, on the way in, with scrap;
                on the way out, on tiptoe with hunger.

If I had their bird sense I might grasp the architecture
       of their floating cities – twist
            and uplift of the warmer air,
an Archimedes' Screw of moisture, its slow veering
       to the wide and weightless
            like a dervish skirt, its stillness
                with footings in movement and light

… and collapsed by a shift of the cloud-cover, de-
       constructed, and the islands sunk
            like whalebacks into silt
mist, bleats of sonar, bottom-feeding… As if light
       as much as earth or water,
            had a basement, back stairs,
                lift shafts. Privacies.

On Poetic Form: *a short essay*

The form stands in the corner of the room
like a man made of glass. All he can be
is how the light bends through him; he's the way
reflections and refractions play, the zero sum
of its deflections and distractions. *Come
on in*, I say, as if there was a he
to speak to, or an I to speak, or words to say
or any other place to come in from

except time. How many rooms have held, might hold
him, he them – had their decor rearranged
in his impartial gaze? He makes me feel old
and young (not in a good way) and yet... *Chance
it*, he says, silently, and everything is changed.
He never moves, and yet we start to dance.

The Same River: *thirteen variations on Heraclitus*

1

The thing is, Heraclitus,
      that it splashes,
            sometimes sucks
at your ankles or your insurance premium;

could drown you, more or less predictably, in spate.

That much we know, and it affects us
      with that rush
            of the chronic and stuck
insistence of the of-the-moment, its whim

to ignore us, suddenly; the mind

is left stuck
      in its tracks
            where it's trying (poor
mind, it must be lonely) to see

its own footsteps in the soft mud

of the river bank
      (eroding)
            certainty and words
eroding, while in the playground of the light

they're always running off, the others,

in their own games
      (always) and
            yet notwithstanding
(least of all with standing)

the thing   is

2

The thing is, Heraclitus,
     that it eddies,
          turns to catch its own
tail vanishing, or your reflection wound up in it;

that's you drowned, predictably, gone.

That much we know. Does it protect us
     from that rush-
          hour spate of them,
the in-your-face faces of the moment, knowing?

Pity him, the poor mind on the bank still

staring after
     where the ripples seem
          to be going (though
we know, a wave flows nowhere, yet

it flows). His feet, sunk in the soft mud

of the river bank,
     itch to wriggle
          ooze between their toes
while on the parade ground of the light

sensations march by, each saluting

at the podium where who
     knows if the lord high self
          is standing
(or his understudy, understanding)

while the thing, whatever it is   is

3

The thing is, Heraclitus,
        shapes come out of the dark
                fully formed
and yet brief as the breath of a flame –

see it there on the cave wall, flash-

tag, like a forked
        tongue from the furnace
                flue, hell's
teeth. We come out of the glare

of the kiln, its blaze still playing

round us like the saw-
        edge crenellations
                round a migraine
burning out from the blind spot

of which nothing can be said.

Behind it, scorched
        earth, thin
                smoke leaking
from torched bracken; nothing

for it but to wait for rain –

the dry spit
        of the first drop
                hitting dust,
with a hiss: the impact at the heart

where no   thing   is

4

Now here's a thing,
          Heraclitus, a pretty
                    kettle of fish,
my Cornish grandma would have said:

the constant comeuppance of river in spate

in which how can we know which
          of the upsurge and downrush
                    of glints and slickback
shadows of a passing moment is fish,

which a wish for a fish of the mind

that leaves us stuck
          with just the abstract
                    notion trying
to net one certain otherness out

to lie there flapping in the mud –

still less *trout*
          (escaping)
                    or less certain words
(escaping) like *roach*, *tench* or *rudd*

while through the sluicegate of the light

the water-shapes fish
          mould themselves to
                    and are moulded by,
remain, in changing, like a standing

wave, as much a thing   as any is

5

The thing is, Heraclitus,
         that the space
                  between the leaves
or branches seems to hold the river; so

I'm letting these words flow, in spate,

in spite of knowing
         better, into a frame
                  that's made
to look like flow. What's contained,

what's released: that's the question

one can come unstuck
         (deliciously)
                  by asking, day
in, day out, and nights most of all.

For my love, if you're listening,

that's what every
         love song I
                  write (and most
of them are, whatever the occasion)

asks: hold me

enough
         that I'm set free
                  into what I am and
both of us into the space between us,

whatever that thing   that is nothing   is

6

The thing is, Heraclitus,
       neither here
             nor there; if
it was either how could it be what

it is – flow. It is that, in spades...

though what's more proverbially futile
       than that, shovelling
          the river. Mind
you, look at how it loads its moments

into buckets on the millwheel's constantly

bent shoulders,
       creaking back.
          That must be more
than nothing, more than something, a thing

the length of a whole river, of how many

rain clouds – call
       it *force*
            (as you would,
in words and names left us by Norsemen)

– and the wind, sea, jetstream, Gulf Stream,

what's the length
       of that? You might
            as well try to measure
Elsewhere... which is where, if any-

where,   the thing is

7

The thing is, Heraclitus,
    that, given
        and granted,
not one single drop sticks around

to see we're OK. We won't be,

in the long view.
    They glitter on;
        we come back
thirty or fifty years later, slower

to find lads stripped to the buff

and bungee trunks
    still launching
        into free fall
from the same spot, with the same

shouts, as if time stuck, played, replayed

the same leap,
    slowly, in wave
        after wave
like paratroopers emptied out of planes

over only-slightly-varied landscapes,

broadcast seed
    that blossoms
        or erupts in slow
sprays as it hits the ground, their cries

the one unchanging   thing   there is

8

The thing is, Heraclitus,
　　　we're on the side-
　　　　　lines of the action
which is to say, why interfere

with the sleek machinery that seems

to deliver us
　　　gifts? Paint kettle,
　　　　　bottle, parking cone.
The treasures of Merthyr, down the Silk

Route surface of the river to our feet.

Beyond this point,
　　　le déluge, a sound
　　　　　as of a... of a million
Coke cans crushed by an eternal fist:

the weir. The constant swarming

upstream at its glass-
　　　smooth wall
　　　　　like a cinema screen
and no admittance. The bridge

where a frayed rope dangles and

so much depends
　　　on such a detail;
　　　　　we hang
on for dear life to the trust

that some　　　thing　　　really　　　is

9

The thing is, Heraclitus,
        that it's out there,
                wild. I've heard it
snarling down the valley, fed with rains

that it feels like a hunger.

I've heard it rise
        in the night; next morning
                I hardly dared look
to see what fence, what portion

of ground it had taken. Our

ground. Or what
        it had left us
                to dispose of
like its stolen goods.

No wonder we lay down these grids

to... if not to
        contain, or detain
                it, at least to explain...
just to find ourselves caged,

our fingers threaded through the bars

we want to rattle
        calling *It's not us,*
                not guilty, we've
been framed. But who'd believe a story

that begins *Well, m'lud, you see, the thing is...?*

10

The thing is, Heraclitus,
      that it's over
            as soon as, no,
before it strikes us. Each sensation.

Twig mats on the flood beach

like mad basketry,
      incapable of holding
            anything but force-
fields round this trunk, that

boulder. They are not the flood.

Maybe they frame
      it, or its passing
           in the shipwreck
of the seasons – as a starrystarry sky

is a wreckage of light.

Hold my hand
      while we scavenge
           there for signs
and constellations: *Look, that's our*

star! as they say that lovers

(other lovers)
      say… Or lead
           me, keeping our eyes
on the ground, beyond the tidewrack. If

there's any thing I trust   that is

11

The thing is, Heraclitus,
     that it's doing
          (if there's an it
that can be doing the *doing*) my head in;

how every dip into this river leaves me

dripping slightly differently; see
     the dribbling of words
          behind me on the page,
like the tail of semi-amphibious fish-

beast, coelacanth, evolving to mudskipper

with the mind
     on its tracks,
          its slip-slop
footprints in the mud, then on the concrete.

Just a few more steps and they'll be set

for ever in the pavement
     like celebrities'
          at Grauman's Chinese
Theatre, slight shadows on the boulevards of light

they're always after running off down

but we've got them
     fixed, the children
          queuing up for standing
in them, not yet understanding quite how

evanescent   the thing   is

12

The thing is, Heraclitus,
        even what you
                said (they said
you said) is flux. Not quite the same

quote twice. Or else always the same

and different.
        That may
                be your point,
the sameness of the difference. Or

vice versa. The light of the mind

escapes itself, in
        glints, in figments,
                off a colourless
crystal of thought, as off the bevel

of a mirror. As they say, the light

plays, plays
        on / off / over /
                with our surfaces –
the way you'll catch it running up

the under of a tree branch, to the sky.

So much for gravity.
        Because today's
                (always) the big
audition – *Next!* Because the play's

the thing   that is

13

The thing is, Heraclitus,
      things do tend
            – downhill, say:
sic omnia fatis in pejus ruere: Speed

all things to the worse, and backward borne

slip from us;
      that was Virgil
            on the slog of labour
twenty centuries ago. Or call it entropy –

every moment waves goodbye to every other,

unreachable, in all
      directions. No
            wonder we run,
we stretch, we pump a little faster.

Or stop suddenly, heartbeats

still echoing
      in the cave
            acoustic,
(echoing), the light rippling up

contrariwise. No wonder we've painted

the walls with
      beasts, with handprints,
            crude monickers
before we turn back downstream

where the thing   we might call *future* is

(The saying 'You cannot step into the same river twice' survives, like all Heraclitus'
work, only in fragments quoted by other authors, and in several different forms.)

The Margin
(Newport Wetlands)

Between...

the grey-on-grey
                sky (steam

breathed off the power station
           into wisht November)

and the Pulverised-Fly-Ash slurry
settled to a wan grit,

              layer me;

between the shuffle-and-thrill
of reed beds, party

children getting ready for
        Surprise!

and the cool

rococo of the pylons,
           the chitter of voltage

like grasshoppers never
              where you bend to see,

        inter-layer these two

worlds walking, look
and word and look and word and

        silence, me and you;

between the many vague retractions
                    of the tide

(for now, for now) and small
stunned bird cries, tattered flightpaths,

                    archaeology

would lay one day
upon another (centuries-

          old footprints
grubbed up by a spring surge,

                    gone) like leaves;

between the wilderment of reeds, the chink
of coot purpose, and the aboriginal

          and utter industry

of whatever rat or vole or other
                    kestrel-meat

has scratched out and laid at our feet
a fan of bright ash-slurry

          (compensation land,
we call this, offered to the sky

from our leftovers, for what birds
come looking for their lost

flood-fields)

                    as close as we'll get
to a clean start; in the long view

layer me.

Beyond

...the sea wall, haze begins
    at no point we can determine,

distance ever more with us by not being there.

Beyond the margin is more
    of the margin, more intensely,

the heartland of itself, with all the edges

(mud, salt, frayed
    waves, stumps of jetties,

signatures of oil or steam, the water's

fine discriminations, gloss,
    satin or matt, and the birds',

  where to pick in the mud, where not)

in-gathered, like a mere
    flat map projection

or the great grey linen tablecloth

grandmother grabbed by the lugs
    of its corners, the crumbs

of us shaken in, frisked to the doorstep,

flapped into the wind,
    into further dimensions,

distances we couldn't grasp of a world.

Beneath

...the great glum and always-
unravelling knot of weather,
pressure, heat, precipitation,

cloud without visible movement
but a bush of steam arisen
from its chimney leans

from the north – not wind
exactly, more that grey itself
might have an inclination

like us this morning; we walk
to be warm, and to find ourselves
somewhere, lifted clean

out of ourselves, as we watch
for a speck, a spore, a sign,
for the grace of migration,

for a thin far cry that puts us
in our place, this temporary landfall,
brief sweet water, and a little green.

Railway Weeds

Where do they think they are,
                              and who,
this flare-up, free festival, this gypsy wedding

of travelling flora, between track and track and rail
and rail: this clinker desert just outside the window, feet away

every morning in everyone's gaze? This scrag end of scree.
This pole of inaccessibility.
                              It's brackland, out-of-bound-

land, flat mountain, a temperate tundra that's mean
with its nutrients but hey,
                              in the flash

of its season, it's sunlight sucked straight in to pink
and carmine, mauve and sherbet-lemon yellow,

hardly bothering with green.
                              What green there is
is kindling, is tinder already. Whoosh. Half-inchers

of soil, they make their own fortune, for a week or two,
blow-ins and blow-away, no good investments but what

the hell, eh, what better than this: that they'll do it
again and again.

Wetland, Thinking...

I... Well, I wouldn't say 'I', to begin with. If I think, *I* think I am a *we*.

§

Water is only one of the voices, though the most volatile, the most apt to come at you with threat, or gift, or glitter. Earth is the quieter partner. It inheres.

§

And plants, the children of this (shifting, this uneasy) marriage made... if not in heaven, in the actions of the moon? They're what holds us together, all the way from marram grass in sand dunes to the sphagnum moss that feeds on, and feeds itself into, the body of the bog.

§

No one governs the 'we' in 'wetlands'. OK, maybe the moon, but is she really looking, does she really care?

§

We're family, then, born into webs of connection? Root hairs, rhizomes, obligations. Channels worn, entrenchments. The awful relations whom we rub along with after all.

§

You don't know, do you, (ah, this human language) whether this 'we' is the kind including 'you'?

§

Or are we crowds of strangers, jostling in the customs hall, towards border control? The rich melange of voices. Tongues as many as grass. You have to bend down very close to hear.

§

You hope we're a pack, like the old drovers' sleek canny black and white dogs, lolloping their own way home. Those dogs grown to be part of your pack, your purpose, only closer to the ground and to the sheep. You can do business with that.

§

We're not so different from you, maybe – you singular, who call yourself a personality. You too let your memories, your meanings, bank and veer and flow to cohere with their neighbours, following their wingtips, the whole flock of you lightening, darkening, scarfing and furling in flight.

§

What do we want of you? You, who've elected yourself first cousin to the old ones, tide and moon…and yet, so childlike, touching really, the way you gaze into us, wanting to see words like 'want', like 'think, like 'I'. Reflections of your own face in our standing water.

§

But we level with you, all the same.

§

You can do this by taste. This blank page of surface water, where the beasts graze, is it salt or sweet? You could take a sample bottle of it for analysis. Or chance it, to know us that close. Our languages, there, on the tip of your tongue.

Broadleaf Torch Song

You could call it abject, call it
lustful, call it a devotion, how I lay
myself out
        at the sky's feet. All-
consuming. I would carpet the earth,
I would gulp the sun whole

and want more. The sun should worry
about this, the love that thrives
on hunger, the hunger
              that thrives
on its feeding, entropy incarnate,
so where could we end?

    (You say I'm speaking your
    thoughts, human. Why not?
    I'm all reception,
              just as you're
    all talk. Every leaf
    is a listening ear.)

... where but in the steady branching
up inside me, like another tree,
of the hardening fact
        of autumn,
the losing my grip on my green?
I'm my own liability

and I shed it. It's all I can do:
to flare up, to cast myself down,
a rust-bright,
        a flesh
and flame coloured mess,
a crescendo of fall

(and don't you love it,
though you've heard it before
year on year?
        You think
I'm singing your song.
Indeed. *Encore*.)

Descaffolding

First, the cries
      (like birds, but Scouse and Geordie)
          and the clatter, then their four,

five, six tangerine tabards
      and hard hats, their banter,
          their casual truckling with gravity

as it dissolves around them,
      the four-storey tower
          they perch in and unpick,

steel tie by fist-sized tie plucked
      like fruit with a flick; a pole's
          free: to *you!* and it flows,

tipped-slipped from hand
      to hand, one long trickling
          cadence like call-and-response

down to the last heave, the thump
      in the truck. It's Saturday,
          and overtime, but steady

does it; hurry or delay
      could have your hand off and
          there's time in this for joshing

as he flips down pole, joke
      then himself; he pours after it,
          from each by each storey

that's no longer there –
      all this in minutes, as if time
          as well as space were being

deconstructed – our lives, in defter
      hands than ours – to the last
           clash on the neat stack,

grace, the van already revving,
      then a buck and double shrug
           of rattle at the speed bump,

wheel by wheel, and that's
      the sum of it, OK? The sum
           of us. It is. OK.

Specific Instances of Silence

The High Style

like the leisurely scored spark-streak
in the almost evening (intercontinental,
at that altitude):
      end of December,
sun already gone down here

but answering, up there, glint for glint,
confidentially, and no word, not
a whisper
      (long skirts trailing
a rumour of power through high halls

to which we're not admitted), no
hint what this mute nod, steel
to sun, this
         angle of incidence,
this moment's flash-and-fade,
might mean.

*

There is a Kind

of silence that tends to be figured as darkness
         and the kind that tends to light.

*

Spelling Silence

was what grown-ups taught him. He learned young:
that slight nod-frown of meaning.
How he knew that 'cancer' has two Cs.

Not to mention the French, the *Pas devant
les enfants*. Education: how he knew that silence
slipped between one language, or one letter, and the next

was see-through. Was a lens, polished glass
like a paperweight in which floated, very
clear, a tiny sea horse, or a family.

*

Gradually
        the people in the room became aware
of her silence, till it drowned out everything.

*

Not

a click on the phone, no whirr
of off, no whine
of disconnection – just

not. Mid-phrase, half way through a rising
intonation… Null.
And they stand either side of everything

too long unsaid or (the sound of ice:
the fracturing, the creaking floes)
too late to say, or unsay, even if they could.

*

Hush

like a dumb
struck bell, its humming
aftermath, when he stretched back
in the long bath, all the family's clatter
and somebody rattling at the door already

as distant as whale song, as his ears go under,

only his nose out, the water accepting the weight
of his head, the too much in it. Crackling suds
and the sound of his fingertips
wrinkling, as he waits
to see who, one day,
he will be.

*

A Rest

that is anything but – a restless
presence on the stave,
                    like the space of an arch,
the force field mapped inside it, drawn onto the air
with the H-est of pencils... so the phrase,

the movement, the whole symphony
is held
          in a teaspoon of pause, like homeopathy
– rinse, swill and rinse the moment, till it's nothing
but its inclination: what, you could believe, it *knows*.

*

With Every Word

the interviewer did not say, and he
did, he was talking himself one step closer to his fall.

*

4' 33

is anything but nothing. Is a vacuum
abhorred, where the world and its life and all its rush hours rushes in.
Sits down beside you, flustered. At the end
of the performance, stands up. Takes a bow. Becomes its own applause.

*

In the Quaker Meeting

on the radio (and this is not
invention) silence had to be spoken for

by the tick of a clock.
Given a heartbeat

(radio silence being, in its own
dimension, death)

so it could go out live, and come to us.

*

His Letters

        from the front arrived, the censor's blanks
black pits, and she stood on the edge. She must not look.

*

The Moment

when the birds rose, all at once, dust
from a beaten carpet, from all the trees in the square,
without a sound
            and scattered downwind –
you have to imagine the breath of their wings –
the lunch hour people, people at the market stalls,

looked up, a moment's question everywhere
not asked.
        That dog too, that cowered
under the bench at her feet, its inaudible whine,

the crying baby somehow stilled... All this
in the dreams where she's trying to call
a warning, back
           from what the world
knows later, to that moment when the coming
earthquake whispered to the birds, the day before.

*

The Fine Gradations
           of the moment, as the doctor
looked up from his lab results, before she spoke.

*

A Beginning:

You, me, and not simply the word but the word
    that waits to be between us –
the particular and limbered space for it,
    waiting. (This too is an act
of faith: conceive it, how the shudder, chop
    and backwash of the air
we bother, tentatively, too much, might ripple
    out then back in, be in-gathered
to one point, this in-breath, original splash
    in the still pool, mute
word, in which we might find ourselves, this
    singularity.)

*

And Don't Assume

the word is 'love'
or is ours. When any two
    or three or more are gathered,
    then, who knows, maybe
it *is* the Name
    that can't be spoken –
    to which even silence,
still more the word 'silence',
is a noise and yet
    diminishment, the heart of things
    hawking its wares in the street.

*

Newborn,
    the distance from the look of something
drowned in air, to the sputter and stir of her first breath.

*

Agnes Martin

painted silence: this

and this and this... Successive
as skylines in low country, a day's walk to where

you see, beyond, another. Each folded sheet

a near-white swirling, slightly, with a tint,
a tincture: every colour is contained in it

like the silt-life, shreds of weed, each breaking

tip of the tide turns up and over. Laying
this by this. At her further remove

from the chatter of things (not far enough

quite to escape the voices in her head)
she laid the wash of calculation, concentration,

contemplation on, dissolving them

in space. A hundred shades of silence.
Hung them in a white room, white on white.

*

Make No Mistake

: some silence is the chokehold. Power,
                    obviously; sometimes, love.

*

It Comes Between

the *What?*

and the *What's the matter?* and the
You should have said and the
I shouldn't have to
tell you and
the end...

*

The First Winter

of the occupation, we learned to button our coats
of silence tighter. To wear layers of it, more
than we had known we owned.
Even moving became hard

but we learned to conceal that, too.

*

Tintinnabuli (Arvo Pärt)

Seven years
of 'silence', so the textbooks
have it... then a note,

and each one following
so single

as it goes into the space
between, where it is not
extinguished, any more

than light is, that to call that
distance 'silence',

might redeem, maybe, silence itself,
from those who hold it
like a weapon in their fist.

*

Then for an Hour

      they saw only the swoop
and swoop of the oncoming headlights,
wide-eyed as a hunting owl. The sweep
at and, just in time, each time, aside...

      The black holes of the lives
behind those lights, rushing somewhere
quite counter, unknowable, back
in a place where he and she may once have been.

*

If I Could Say

      now what those tears meant
they would be muddied. Let the water speak.

*

One Heresy

holds that before
the light there was the listening,
a more than silence:

readiness
already shaped and resonant,
tingling – before the word
(read on with care, this
is the heresy)
the bright acoustic – to receive us
and return us clearer,
all our jangled wavelengths,
us, the sun, the other stars.

*

And at One of Those Moments

when we're running into words
towards each other, we might think,

and yet it thickens, thickets deepening:
a hunt by night... this something

else is with us, as sharp as the crack
of a twig giving way under no

greater weight than moonlight: this
equal-and-opposite, this most particular

silence, the shape of the word we will
persist in thinking that *we only have to say*.

*

In the Grand Opera

of silence, there are arias, and the tiresome recitative,
                    and then, beneath it all, the music.

Habitation

It's not the stone,
                    the slate flagged floor
beneath the cross-stitched sampler, but
the four-hundred-year tread,
uneven. Daily.
                    Bread. Our trespasses.
It's not the pattern in the carpet but
the wear – the bare threads,
jute, hemp,
                    showing through:
the one
          prayer I who don't pray have
by habit – not the words, their
crumbling in translation,
pollen to the touch,
                    dust of butterfly wings,
but the flow of it, the ebb, like the creak
on the turn of the stairs, a familiar step
that stumbles, is it,
                    or the pause
for breath?
          Some nights I breathe it
merely, just its hesitancy, happening
into rhythm now and then.
Let it rest
          there, on a weak beat,
without (added later)
power and glory
– leave it near
                    the time of trial or
Deliver us...
          A breath-shape
rising in the cold air. Fading
slowly. Habitation.

It's not mine
　　　　and God knows
it's not much
　　　　　but it'll serve.

Fratres: **Permutations on Arvo Pärt**

Let this be the tension, then,
of stillness. Audibly. The shiver
    of sensations like the twitch
    of metal cooling, on the surface

        of the mind. The body, still
        enough to hear its own
unstillness. This you might
call prayer. A breath,

    the longest, on the surface
    of the sky: the tensile strings
        of cirrus, wind-quiver
        in the long grass

from horizon to horizon
and the wires that slightly
differently sag from each
pole to each regular pole

beside the rail track. This
is listening for the turn:
        the wires alter their tone;
        birds, gathering, bothering

    briefly, flake off into flight,
    each with its momentary
hesitation, south. This makes it
not a less but more sure thing.

    this, daily: waking to the early
    dark, one step after the other,
    shambling into place again
    inside one's self, one's self

in the foursquare cloister,
the four seasons – *fratres* –
in the sound of sandalled feet,
a little sore, on stone, and cold.

This is the boat's wake
widening behind until
it is wider than the bay.
the land diminishing. This

is the creaking of flight feathers
finding purchase on unwieldy air

somehow, together. Taking hold.

Applause, Applause

Why not start from the end

where the edifice of sound and space,
acoustics and attention, (whatever the concert hall
or slack marquee we're in)

begins to crumble

                with a sound like running scree

                    then crashes? Is collapsed
           by us all: the pillars of the temple. Necessary
                consummation. All together now.

                  Let's bring it clattering down.

Almost too obvious,

the glory-fallout from a brassy climax.
More telling, that out of a Lied von der Erde
ewig! ewig! or a Lark-Arising-

out-of-hearing long slow fade:

                  expectancy, how long before

                the rainstorm. Ritual thrashing
          of the flat roofs, of the pavement, sparks
                leaping up to the streetlight,

              flash flood made with two dry palms

together, all together.

Clapping solo would be pathos.
Or sarcasm. Rather have the silence
filling up to the horizon,

meadows full of fallen sky.

But we aren't ready for that.

That comes later. Now, we raise
the roof (of whatever church or school hall,
the caretaker yawning at the door)

and bring the house down,

.

on our feet now, an uprising

in spite of ourselves
victorious,
loosing volleys in the air

in the ruins of silence, the rubble of sound.

Blackbird, Descending

(for MJAG, 1915-2005)

(Chris Hughes, Slow Motion Blackbird: 'Very gradually slow down a recorded sound to many times its original length without changing its pitch or timbre...' Steve Reich 9/67)

1

One loop of what it pleases us
to call song:
           how the bird we don't see
writes itself into space, its signature
on time.
          This once. Again, and
slower now, and then
slower again

as if this might be all there is:
enough. It might be that we need to look no further.

2

Each loop of slowing: each turn of the stair. Each
deeper: it lowers you down inside itself
through galleries
of sound. Grow up in Cornwall, and you'll know this
hollow feeling, nearby, you might not
know where:
among the bracken, suddenly, a fenced-off bramble patch
leans inward, over something it's not
saying, that you have to
lob a stone to hear. Shafts, with chambers opening back
to workings, darkness, glints of wet
rock, glints of ore.
The creaking of the winding gear – which may be
what all our vibrations, note and syllable,
come down to: the man-engine,

winching us down as far as we have breath to go.

3

I'll say the word because it's present
            for the saying: *fractal* –
a word you would have shied from, Jay:
            too clever for me.
Wrong. Watch it shiver into smallness
            like the ripples, out
then inwards, endless, from the splash
            in a drowned mine.
What's it like there, tell me, in eternity?

4

I wonder now whether it could ever sleep,
the bird body and bones that kept giving
            and giving it, filling

the open-and-lit-at-all-hours ambulance bay
the sliding doors released their one breath onto,
            where I stepped into a new
                        sense of the night

after the three a.m. call and the rush across town
too late, the slow steps to the bedside – can I
            touch? – to touch

your hand, already cooling. But the bird,
the one filling its sodium dawn with what
            you wouldn't mind my calling
                        glory...

how would it ever get to sleep, poor thing?

5

Each note opens inwards, slowing,
into intrications of itself. Unsuspected
timbres, trills as fine as root-hairs,
the brilliant subtleties
                         you never thought
you had. The bird itself, in the end,
might be astonished, looking into its own song,
flutter-ruffling in,
                    to be lost
as in a great wood (as we all are, listening)
– to find it as familiar as strange.

6

Imagine this
                in a dugout, waiting for the order.
In a doorway in a shrapnel-raddled wall,

a short and only sprint down sniper's alley –
how close this might be to enough,

as if you heard a whole life in it; it might utter you.

Or any hushed room we might come to, just before,
or after, is it, the breath, can you tell? Indifferent

procedures, sounds off, going on outside the door –
the corridor, the lift shaft – or outside the window. What

you might take for a blackbird, in what it might take for Spring.

Written on Light

Beyond the pier this morning,
a pure dazzle – only, in it, silently,

the come and go of white sails,
right to left and left to right.

translucent, barely distinct
from the depthlessness they move in

– slight geometries and intersections
of it in the stillness, just perceptibly

filling or flexing. Beyond our gravity
there are craft (there are, already)

that ride on the breath of the sun,
the mere pressure of light.

*

      Just come
into its own, the day,
      the twice-
times sun, the sum

of suns, it and its own
      reflection
on the sea. Its self-
      sufficiency.

*

Such a delicate cusp
this evening: the sky,
the sea
            and the barely
discernible hinge between them.

No, I don't believe
in Judgement but yes,
we will be held
            to account.
Like this. In every detail.

Held, that is, as in a rare
find, fine china, the one of itself,
with its flaws, held
            gently and exactly.
Held up, to be filled with light